P9-CJS-275

on the radar

being
a stunt
performer

Isabel Thomas

Lerner Publications Company
Minneapolis

First American edition published in 2013 by Lerner Publishing Group, Inc. Published by arrangement with Wayland, a division of Hachette Children's Books

Copyright © 2012 by Wayland

Lerner Publications Company
A division of Lerner Publishing Group, Inc.
241 First Avenue North
Minneapolis, MN U.S.A.

Website address: www.lernerbooks.com

Library of Congress
Cataloging-in-Publication Data

Thomas, Isabel, 1980–
    Being a stunt performer / by Isabel Thomas.
       p.   cm. — (On the radar: awesome jobs)
    Includes index.
    ISBN 978-0-7613-7776-4 (lib. bdg. : alk. paper)
    1. Stunt performers—Juvenile literature. 2. Stunt performers—Vocational guidance—Juvenile literature.
    I. Title.
    PN1995.9.S7T45   2013
    791.4302'8—dc23   2011052663

Manufactured in the United States of America
    – CG – 7/15/12

Acknowledgements: Alamy: AF archive 21, Interfoto 20–21; Corbis: David Appleby/Buena Vista Pictures/Bureau L.A. Collection 14; Paul Darnell: 2b, 30–31; Dreamstime: Ben Heys 11, 19b, Linqong 19c, Marion Wear 13; Flickr: B Furlong 7, Rob Young 8–9; iStock: Greg Epperson 6b, Jurie Maree cover; Rex: Mike Forster/Daily Mail 16–17; Luci Romberg: 2t, 24–25, 25bc; Shutterstock: Eniko Balogh 4–5, 22, 28–29, Helga Esteb 23, Germanskydiver 25br, Mayskyphoto 10–11, Christophe Michot 2–3, Gabi Moisa 1, PJ Morley 25bl, Jordan Tan 3br, 19t; Mark Wagner: c, 26; Wikipedia: 12, Luc Viatour 18r.

Main body text set in
Helvetica Neue LT Std 13/15.5.
Typeface provided by Adobe Systems.

cover stories

the**people**

the**moves**

the**talk**

THE REAL ACTION STARS!

Action stars such as Taylor Lautner and Angelina Jolie are famous for their exciting films, in which they leap from exploding cars, hang from helicopters, and rappel down skyscrapers. So, how do they do it? The fact is, in most cases, they don't. Stunt performers stand in for them. While these tough professionals perform seemingly impossible feats, the A-list stars may be enjoying a beverage in their trailers!

To the extreme

Stuntmen and stuntwomen are highly skilled, world-class athletes. Their job is to do dangerous things in a safe way so that they look amazing on-screen. These stunt doubles step in for main characters when things get tough.

Risky business

Stunt sequences are carefully planned to make them as safe as possible. However, stuntmen and stuntwomen have to take risks. They must perform moves over and over, until they look just right on-screen. From bruises to broken bones, injuries are all part of a day's work.

Professional hero

Years of training and experience are needed to become a stunt performer. After all, stunt teams only want to work with people who can perform feats safely. Stunt professionals travel to amazing locations, work with stars, and see themselves on-screen. No two jobs are the same, so they are unlikely to be bored. Best of all, they do what they love and get paid for it!

Action all-arounders

A stuntperson's job does not end on a film set.
Performers must train each day to keep their bodies in
excellent condition. They also need to practice different
activities. For example, they must be good at combat
sports such as martial arts and boxing. They must excel
in gymnastics, trampolining, and high diving. They must
be adept at outdoor sports such as swimming, horseback
riding, motor racing, free running, and rock climbing.

STUNT SPEAK

Use the On the Radar guide to learn the lingo and sound like a stunt pro.

air bag
a bag filled with air to cushion high falls and collisions

air ram
a piece of equipment used in stunts to flip vehicles or people into the air

CGI
computer-generated imagery, such as fireballs, that are created with software and added to scenes in films

choreograph
to plan a series of moves for the performance of a dance or stunt

free climbing
climbing without using fixed safety ropes

free running
a sport like parkour, with extra acrobatics and creativity

full-body burn
when a stuntperson moves through a wall of fire

parkour
a sport that involves running, jumping, and climbing over obstacles in an urban area

rappel
to travel down a vertical surface using a rope

second-unit director
the director of stunts and other shots not involving the stars in a film

set
scenery built for a play, TV show, or film

stage combat
a harmless fighting technique used by actors to look like real fighting

stunt coordinator
an experienced stuntman or stuntwoman who plans and oversees stunts

stunt double
also called a body double; a stuntman or stuntwoman who stands in for an actor, performing as a particular character in the film

stunt sequence
a carefully planned set of moves, tricks, or stunts that are filmed in one take

Stuntpeople are trained to carry out dangerous free-climbing moves.

take
a scene filmed without stopping the camera

Taurus World Stunt Awards
an award ceremony held each year for stunt professionals

wire
a wire to which a stuntperson is connected to ensure his or her safety

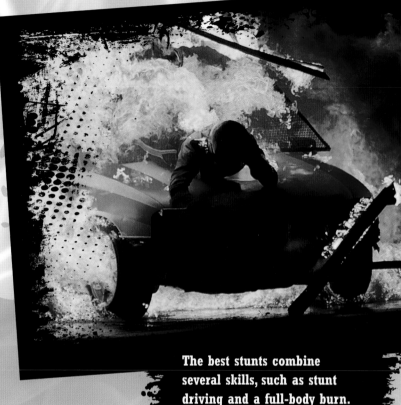

The best stunts combine several skills, such as stunt driving and a full-body burn.

GLOSSARY

adrenaline
a hormone found in the human body that causes the heart to beat faster

clapboard
a device used at the start of a film or TV scene. It makes a noise that helps to coordinate the pictures and sound during editing.

dedication
commitment to a task

endurance
the ability to get through something difficult without giving up

kung fu
a Chinese martial art

name-check
to mention someone by name

pro
short for professional; someone who is paid to perform stunts

semitruck
a large truck with a cab attached to one or more trailers

trilogy
a series of three, for instance, three films

FALL OUT!

You're standing on the roof of a ten-story building. Your heart pounds as you walk toward the edge. The dizzying drop makes your stomach lurch. Your body says run away, but your brain tells you to keep going. You're a tough stunt professional, and you've been hired to jump off the roof in a ball of flames.

And action!

Your eyes lock on the air bag below. From about 100 feet (30 meters) up, it looks just as hard as the pavement. The cast and crew scurry around like an army of ants, making last-minute checks on the cameras pointed in your direction. They are relying on you. You begin psyching yourself up for the jump. The assistant tells you to prepare for a blaze that is about to light up your bodysuit. You've done it before, but every time feels like the first. If it goes wrong, you could really hurt yourself. The second-unit director shouts, "Roof Jump. Take 1. Action!" The slap of the clapboard is your cue to leap.

The rush

Your heart races as you fall downward. You can feel the heat on your back from the fire, while air rushes past your face like a jet stream. All you can see is the ground rushing toward you! Your training kicks in, and you control your body for a safe landing. Bang! You hit the air bag, but the adrenaline rushing through your veins means you barely feel the impact.

It's a wrap

As you roll onto the solid ground, the safety team members cover you in a froth of foam. The fire is out, and a round of applause ripples around the set. Everyone's happy with the take, and you know that it will look great on the big screen. The reaction from the cast and crew is the best. You're part of an awesome team. Nothing beats the thrill of a day's work.

FIREBALL

Stunts involving fire can add breathtaking drama to a film. However, they are extremely dangerous and are performed only by a highly experienced team.

Essential preparation

- Full safety checks
- Fire and ambulance crew on standby
- Precision timing

Why do it?

Stuntpeople can add an authenticity to a fire scene that cannot be created by a computer. However, the stunt is a high-risk procedure that requires hours of careful planning and strenuous safety checks to ensure that nothing goes wrong.

How it's done

1. The stunt performer puts on several layers of fire-resistant clothing, including a special protective hood and gloves.

2. The stunt coordinating team checks that the protective clothing fully covers the stuntperson so that no flesh will be exposed to the flames.

3. The stunt coordinating team then coats the stuntperson in a flammable gel.

4. The team signals to the camera crew and director that they can start filming.

5. The flammable gel is lit, and the action sequence is filmed. Throughout the scene, the stuntperson wears a face mask through which he or she can safely breathe.

6. The stunt coordinating team puts out the flames and checks that the stunt performer is unharmed.

JAW-DROPPING ACTS

Long before filmmakers needed stunt professionals, daredevils performed stunts for excited and shocked crowds. Trapeze artists, sword swallowers, and extraordinary horse riders have pulled crowds to circus shows for hundreds of years. History is packed with the thrills and spills of stunt performances.

One of Houdini's most famous stunts was his Handcuff Challenge, in which he escaped from chains around his hands, feet, and neck.

The Great Houdini

Harry Houdini was one of the first people to turn stunts into entertainment. In the late-1800s, his impossible escapes and endurance tricks made him one of the world's most popular entertainers. In the early 1900s, he appeared in some of the very first silent movies, becoming one of Hollywood's first action heroes.

Death plunge

Thrill seekers around the world followed Houdini's lead and tried to become rich and famous by performing stunts. Many have plunged over North America's most powerful waterfall, the thunderous Niagara Falls. The first to succeed was a 63-year-old woman who dreamed of being famous. Annie Taylor (1838–1921) made the 177-foot (54 m) drop in a wooden barrel in 1901—and survived! Several people have died attempting to copy her feat.

Higher, farther, faster

Fast-moving motor vehicles gave stunt performers a new way to wow the crowds. Evel Knievel (1938–2007) became famous for leaping his motorbike over cars, buses, trucks, and even canyons. Airplanes were also used for adrenaline-fueled stunts. The U.S. Navy's Blue Angels and the U.S. Air Force's Thunderbirds are world-famous aerobatic display teams. They carry out daring displays in superfast jets.

Real-life action hero

Some of the most exhilarating stunts are not done for money or fame but for the challenge. In 1974 Philippe Petit shocked the world by stringing a steel cable between the towers of New York's World Trade Center and walking across it without a safety harness! He made the trip—an incredible 1,300 feet (396 m) from the ground—eight times. Another Frenchman, Alain Robert, makes headlines by free climbing the world's tallest buildings.

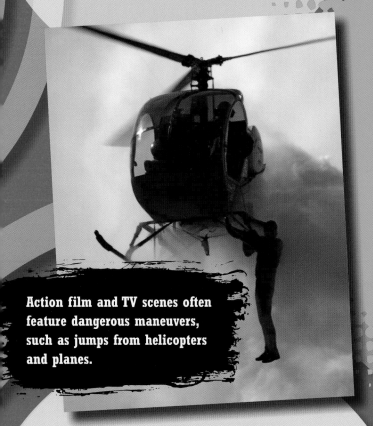

Action film and TV scenes often feature dangerous maneuvers, such as jumps from helicopters and planes.

Fantastic film stunts

Beginning in the 1960s, new technology helped film stunts become bigger, better, and more realistic. Air bags allowed stunt performers to fall from enormous heights. Air rams helped stunt teams create breathtaking car chases. Stunt coordinators and performers continue to perfect techniques and equipment, and every year, more daring and inventive stunts keep audiences glued to the screen.

JACKIE CHAN

Superstar stuntman

Jackie performs one of his legendary martial arts stunts in *Around the World in 80 Days* (2004).

Career highlights

1962 landed his first acting role at eight years old in *Seven Little Valiant Fighters*

1979 directed his first movie, *Fearless Hyena*

2001 starred in *Rush Hour 2*: one of the most successful martial arts films ever made

2008 voiced a monkey in the hit animation *Kung Fu Panda*

2010 starred in the blockbuster, *The Karate Kid*

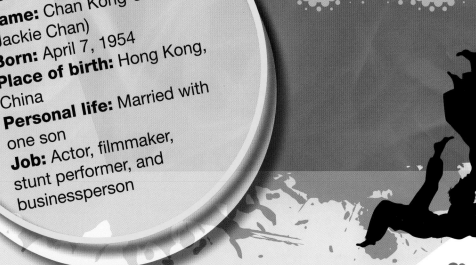

THE STATS
Name: Chan Kong-sang (Jackie Chan)
Born: April 7, 1954
Place of birth: Hong Kong, China
Personal life: Married with one son
Job: Actor, filmmaker, stunt performer, and businessperson

Kung fu kid

Jackie's passion for martial arts began when he was very young. Every morning, he got up early to practice kung fu with his dad. When Jackie was seven, his parents enrolled him in Hong Kong's China Drama Academy. He spent 10 years learning martial arts, acrobatics, and acting but was never taught to read and write. (He memorizes his lines.)

Stunt star

In his late teens, Jackie began to win stunt roles in Chinese-language martial arts films. He would try anything. His fearless attitude impressed Hong Kong filmmakers. When he was 21, Jackie landed his first starring role, in *New Fist of Fury*. He was full of creative ideas and liked to introduce new stunts and comedy into his martial arts films. Jackie became a big star in Asia.

"Superstunt" king

Jackie's ultimate dream was to be a global superstar, which meant making films in Hollywood. His big break came when he made the hit film *Rumble in the Bronx* (1995). Jackie's sensational "superstunt" expertise caught the eye of Hollywood film producers. He soon made many more Hollywood films and became a sought-after A-list star.

Hole in the head

Audiences loved Jackie's carefully choreographed superstunts, but they were risky. Jackie was injured many times. He was almost killed when he jumped from a castle wall onto a tree and fell to the ground. The impact made a hole in his skull, and Jackie underwent immediate surgery. He still has the hole in his head.

Global empire

Jackie has used his fame to help charities and start many businesses, including a stunt school. He still makes films, but now he is so famous that he uses stunt doubles himself! He takes roles in many different types of films, saying, "I want all the audience to know that not only can I fight, I can really act."

GLASS FALL

The glass fall is a dramatic stunt in which a stunt performer smashes through a window or glass door to simulate a fall or a jump. This dangerous stunt can result in severe cuts if performed badly, so only the most experienced stunt performers attempt it.

Essential preparation

- Stunt coordinators ensure windows and doors are fitted with breakaway or tempered glass.
- Protective clothing is worn.
- Has lots of nerve!

Why do it?

Scenes in which actors fall or are pushed through glass make exciting viewing. With the use of special glass, these stunts can look extremely convincing. However, crashing through glass is very risky and should be done only by a fully trained stunt professional.

HOW IT'S DONE

1. Two types of glass are used: tempered and breakaway. They both break more easily than standard glass upon impact. Tempered glass shatters into sharp pieces, while breakaway glass falls to the ground as small blunt pieces.

2. If working with tempered glass, the stuntperson puts on a protective bodysuit.

3. A member of the stunt team called an FX person stands ready to activate a device that triggers the break in the glass. The FX person and stuntperson must time the moves perfectly. Otherwise, the tempered glass will break before the stuntperson falls through it!

4. Breakaway glass can be broken by the performer, which makes it less dangerous and easier to use.

TRICKS OF THE TRADE

Dramatic car crashes, fearsome fight scenes, and extreme explosions electrify the big screen. Stunt teams use technical tricks to capture dangerous-looking action, while ensuring that performers stay as safe as possible.

Look before you leap

Stuntmen and stuntwomen put their lives in the hands of stunt coordinators, who plan and prepare each stunt. Before anyone leaps off a building or drives a car off a bridge, safety measures are put in place based on careful calculations. The next step is to rehearse the stunt meticulously.

Staged fight!

Stunt fighters use a well-rehearsed sequence of moves to create a performance that looks just like an actual fight. All stunt fights are carefully performed so that the stuntpeople are not actually hurt.

Computer wizards

Computer-generated imagery or special effects help to make film and TV stunts safer. Lifelike explosions, floods, fires, and fights can be added as computer graphics. Safety equipment, such as cables and air bags, can be removed from the final pictures.

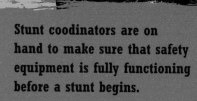

Stunt coodinators are on hand to make sure that safety equipment is fully functioning before a stunt begins.

However, no stunt is risk-free. Every year, many stuntmen and stuntwomen are injured, and some are killed. Stunt coordinators like to work only with people they trust to train hard and follow instructions. This makes the industry very hard to get into.

Stunt car chases are rehearsed for weeks or even months to ensure that nothing goes wrong during filming.

Stuntpeople rehearse routines made up of punches and kicks that do not actually harm the other person, although they seem to on-screen.

Many of the dramatic effects seen in action films, such as explosions, are CGI magic. CGI artists add explosions and flames to a stunt after it has been filmed.

STUNT STARS

These outstanding stunt professionals have performed some of the most amazing feats ever seen on-screen.

1. Joe Canutt

This incredible stuntman could have been killed when he was flipped out of a racing chariot (*right*) being pulled by four galloping horses in the film *Ben Hur* (1959). Instead, the brave stunt double pulled himself out of the path of the thundering hooves and back onto the chariot to finish filming the scene! The stunt was directed by Joe's dad, Yakima Canutt, who was world-famous for his death-defying stunts in films such as *Stagecoach* (1939).

2. Simon Crane

During a hijack scene in the film *Cliffhanger* (1993), stuntman Simon Crane performed one of the world's most dangerous and expensive stunts: sliding down a cable between two flying airplanes. The film's star, Sylvester Stallone, is reported to have cut his fee by $1 million to pay for this amazing scene.

3. Gary Powell

James Bond films are famous for their daring stunts. Gary Powell topped previous Bond chase scenes by flipping a speedboat into a 360-degree spin in *The World Is Not Enough* (1999). If the boat had landed on its roof, his head would have been ripped off. The 15-minute chase took a total of seven weeks to shoot on the Thames River in London, England.

4. Michelle Yeoh

This incredible stuntwoman is one of a few actresses who performs her own stunts. In *Supercop* (1992), she pulled off one of the most dangerous stunts ever done by a woman: jumping a dirt bike onto the roof of a moving train. She was then cast as a Bond girl in *Tomorrow Never Dies* (1997) and became a Hollywood star. Michelle went on to wow audiences in the film *Crouching Tiger, Hidden Dragon* (2000), in which she performed dazzling fight scenes and stunts.

5. Wayne Michaels

The amazing bungee jump off a 750-foot-high (229 m) dam performed by Wayne Michaels in *GoldenEye* (1995) is one of the most famous James Bond stunts. The bungee cord had to be exactly the right length. Too long and he would hit the ground. Too short and he would risk bouncing against the lethal steel rods that covered the dam wall. As he hurtled toward the ground, Wayne calmly acted the part of Bond reaching for a gun.

50 CAL.

ROCKETS

LANDING THE PRIZE

Stuntmen and stuntwomen are calling for their work to be recognized with Hollywood's top prize—an Academy Award.

An Oscar category for Best Stunt Coordination was suggested in 1999. Although the Academy rejected the idea in 2005, campaigners hope it may still be accepted one day.

The ultimate award

The awards, known as Oscars, are handed out every year to the film industry's top people, from actors to makeup artists. Yet despite doing the most dangerous work on a film set, stunt performers have no Oscar awards category. (The Taurus World Stunt Awards are aimed at recognizing excellence in this area.)

Hollywood's heroes

The campaign to recognize Hollywood's unsung heroes began over 20 years ago. Famous filmmakers, including Steven Spielberg and Martin Scorsese, have shown their support. Stuntmen and stuntwomen have thrilled fans of the most famous Oscar-winning films, from *Titanic* (1997) to the *Lord of the Rings* trilogy (2001–2003). Many feel that without stunt performers, action films would be boring.

Keeping it special

The Academy of Motion Picture Arts and Sciences rarely adds new awards. It is worried that too many categories will make the Oscars less special. However, in 1967, a one-off Oscar was awarded to stuntman Yakima Canutt for his lifetime of remarkable work. Stunt coordinator Ken Bates also won a special prize in 1993. Several groups now say that there should be an annual award for people who risk their lives on camera.

Red carpet roll call

Despite the calls to provide them with an Academy category, many stunt professionals are happy to stay out of the spotlight. They believe their job is to make the audience think that its favorite actor is racing a car or winning a fight. But if other members of the profession are successful in their bid to be recognized at the Oscars, the on-set action heroes may find themselves standing side by side on the red carpet with their film-star doubles!

LUCI "STEEL" ROMBERG

On the Radar expert Luci Romberg is a champion gymnast, free runner, and a leading Hollywood stuntwoman. She tells On the Radar what it's like to work in film, TV, and live shows.

How did you get into stunts?

When I was in college, one of my gymnastics teammates began doing acting and stunts. She convinced me to try it. It wasn't easy. It took years of hard work and dedication. You also need a bit of luck to meet people who will give you jobs.

What is the most dangerous stunt you've performed?

Rolling underneath a semitruck that was going at 31 miles (50 kilometers) per hour!

Do you feel scared when you perform?

Film and TV stunts are well planned. So far, I have always felt safe because I trust the people around me. If I don't have the skills for a particular job, I'll turn it down and recommend someone else. I am smart about accepting my limits and not taking unnecessary risks.

What films and TV shows have you worked on?

I've performed stunts in more than 40 films and TV shows, such as *Indiana Jones and the Kingdom of the Crystal Skull* (2008) and *Green Lantern* (2011).

What do you do when you're not shooting a film or TV show?

As well as working in film and TV, many stunt pros work in live shows. I play Peter Pan in a live show at Disneyland. A pirates' ship is my office. What's cooler than that?!

How do you keep fit?

I do free running, hiking, biking, running, and boxing.

Have you ever been injured?

I've been really lucky so far. I've only had small injuries such as painful knees, sprained ankles, and broken fingers.

What advice do you have for someone wanting to become a stuntperson?

Train hard—you will need to reach a professional standard in several sports to do this job. Never give up, and don't let *anyone* tell you that you can't do something!

ACTION HERO

My story by Mark Wagner

I grew up doing gymnastics and drama classes. Then I started to perform circus acrobatics with the world-famous Cirque du Soleil. I met some stunt pros who all told me my background was perfect for stunt work, so I decided to give it a try.

My big break was in *Spider-Man* (2002). I got to perform major stunts in front of important people in the movie business. The most dangerous was a scene in which Spider-Man dives off a bridge to save Mary Jane and a tram full of children. I had to fall about 20 feet (6 m) toward rocks with a stuntwoman attached to me!

The hardest and most unusual stunt I've ever pulled is a sword fight on top of a huge, rolling wheel in *Pirates of the Caribbean: Dead Man's Chest* (2006). We spent three months figuring out how to make it happen. We ended up running backward on a 16-foot (5 m) wheel, while fighting, with only a small wire to catch us if we fell. That scene won me my second Taurus World Stunt Award for Best Fight.

I've been lucky enough to avoid big injuries, but I've had many bumps and bruises. In one fight scene, I was hit in the face by a wooden plank and needed over 30 stitches in and around my mouth!

I love performing wire stunts, and my dream stunt is the decelerator— jumping off a high building with a wire attached. My advice to anyone wanting to follow in my footsteps is to train hard, know your abilities, and do your research. It's a long road, but the payoff is pretty awesome.

NO LIMITS

Pro stuntmen and stuntwomen pushed their minds and bodies to the limit to carry out these world-beating stunts.

Must be Maddo

Who: Robbie (Maddo) Maddison
When: March 29, 2008
Where: Melbourne, Australia
What: Longest ramp jump on a motorcycle
How: Maddo launched his bike 351 feet (107 m) through the air.

Jumping Jacquie

Who: Jacquie de Creed
When: 1983
Where: Santa Pod Raceway, England
What: Long-distance car ramp jump
How: Stuntwoman Jacquie became world-famous when she rocketed 232 feet (71 m) through the air in a 1969 Ford Mustang.

Champion survivor

Who: Evel Knievel
When: 1938–2007
Where: United States
What: Most bones broken in a stunt career
How: Daredevil Knievel broke 37 different bones in his body during his stunt career.

Tumbling Travis

Who: Travis Pastrana
When: 2006
Where: Summer X Games in Los Angeles, California
What: Motorcycle backflips
How: Pastrana became the first person to successfully complete a double backflip on a motorcycle in competition.

Start your engine

Who: Tanner Foust
When: 2011
Where: Indianapolis, Indiana
What: Longest jump in a four-wheel-drive vehicle
How: Foust, a movie stunt driver, launched an SUV outfitted to look like a Hot Wheels car 332 feet (107 m) through the air at the festivities for the 100th annual Indy 500.

Lucky seven

Who: Adam Kirley
When: 2006
Where: Set of James Bond film *Casino Royale*
What: Most car rolls in a single take
How: Stunt double Kirley rolled an Aston Martin seven times in a dramatic car crash scene.

Body burn

Who: Keith Malcolm
When: July 5, 2009
Where: Hampshire, England
What: Longest distance run while on fire
How: Malcolm ran 259 feet (79 m) with his body on fire. He wore protective clothing but no breathing gear.

Speed Kitty

Who: Kitty O'Neill
When: 1976
Where: Alvord Desert in Oregon
What: Set the land-speed record for the quarter mile
How: Deaf stuntwoman Kitty O'Neil drove a quarter of a mile (0.4 km) in 3.22 seconds in a car fueled by hydrogen peroxide.

PAUL DARNELL

THE STATS

Name: Paul "Diddy" Darnell (right)
Born: March 17, 1976
Place of birth: Gloucester, Virginia
Home: Los Angeles, California
Job: Stunt professional and free-running legend

Jumping into stunts

As a teenager, Paul loved watching the creative stunts in Jackie Chan films. Soon Paul realized that he wanted to perform stunts for a living. In 2007 he moved to Los Angeles and founded his own free running and parkour group, called Tempest. His goal was to "push the limits of what is physically possible and add some style to it." Training was fun and an amazing workout, so Paul kept getting better and better. After Tempest performed at the Taurus World Stunt Awards in 2007, Paul began landing stunt jobs in movies.

Passion for life

Paul has become a star himself. In 2011 he performed in the hit film *Water for Elephants* and starred in a new TV show called *Jump City*. He has also opened the Tempest Academy, where people can learn stunt skills. Paul's passion for life is summed up by his own motto. "Explore your world . . . set goals and *never* pass on a once-in-a-lifetime opportunity."

Sporty start

As a child, Paul loved doing anything physical. He played basketball, baseball, and tennis at school. His weekends were filled with everything from break dancing to BMX riding. He and his friends even made up a sport called XJ (extreme jumping). When Paul saw a TV show about parkour, he realized that there were people out there doing XJ using professional techniques. He was on a mission to find out more about the extreme sport.

Twilight fever

Paul's amazing moves won him the role of stunt double to one of Hollywood's hottest stars, Robert Pattinson (*above left*), in the *Twilight* films of 2008 and 2011. Paul hit the headlines when Robert name-checked him as Robert collected an MTV Movie Award for Best Fight.

GET MORE INFO

Books

Horn, Geoffrey M. *Movie Stunts and Special Effects*. New York: Gareth Stevens Publishing, 2006. This book gives an overview of stunts used in movies.

Mason, Paul, and Sarah Eason. *Free Running*. Minneapolis: Lerner Publications Company, 2012. Explore how this extreme sport has made its way into the movies.

Thomas, William David. *Movie Stunt Worker*. Tarrytown, NY: Marshall Cavendish, 2010. In this book, readers follow a movie stunt crew as they set up and execute stunts.

Wolf, Steve. *The Science behind Movie Stunts & Special Effects*. New York: Skyhorse Publishing, 2007. Stuntman Wolf shows how knowledge of science and math is essential for creating safe stunts.

Websites

How Stuff Works—Stunts
**http://entertainment.howstuffworks
.com/stuntmen.htm**
This website describes the ins-and-outs of the lives of stunt performers.

PBS—Stuntwomen
**http://www.pbs.org/independentlens/
doubledare/stuntwomen.html**
PBS discusses women in the film stunt industry.

Taurus World Stunt Awards
**http://www.taurusworldstuntawards
.com/**
Check out this website to learn about what films are being recognized for their quality stunt work.

INDEX